1 MONTH OF
FREE
READING

at

www.ForgottenBooks.com

By purchasing this book you are eligible for one month membership to ForgottenBooks.com, giving you unlimited access to our entire collection of over 1,000,000 titles via our web site and mobile apps.

To claim your free month visit: www.forgottenbooks.com/free38385

ISBN 978-0-483-58595-9
PIBN 10038385

This book is a reproduction of an important historical work. Forgotten Books uses
state-of-the-art technology to digitally reconstruct the work, preserving the original format
whilst repairing imperfections present in the aged copy. In rare cases, an imperfection in
the original, such as a blemish or missing page, may be replicated in our edition. We do,
however, repair the vast majority of imperfections successfully; any imperfections that
remain are intentionally left to preserve the state of such historical works.

M2--5--2

A THEORY OF INDUSTRIAL LIBERTY

by

WILLIAM MONROE BALCH

A Thesis submitted for the degree of

MASTER OF LETTERS

UNIVERSITY OF WISCONSIN

1898.

"But those exertions of the natural liberty of a few
individuals, which might endanger the security of the whole
society, are, and ought to be, restrained by the laws of all
government; of the most free as well as of the most despotical."

Adam Smith.

"Liberty is indeed a great good, but we must submit to
restrictions upon our liberty- even for the sake of liberty."

Richard T. Ely.

Introduction.

Centuries of history have been marching to the drum-beat of liberty. Says John Stuart Mill: "The struggle between Liberty and Authority is the most conspicuous feature in the portions of history with which we are earliest familiar, particularly in that of Greece, Rome and England."*

In his essay on "Liberty", the same author regards his subject primarily from a political standpoint. Up to the present century political interests (though indistinguishably associated with religious interests), were at the forefront both in the actual life and written records of history. Simply because those times had been the ages chiefly of "arms and the man", the struggle had been chiefly a matter of the constitutions and institutions of states.

Then came the new epic and the new era of "tools and the man".+ "The time was when the history of a people was but the history of its government. It is otherwise now."§ Politics and religion mean no less to us than to other generations, but the nineteenth century takes its peculiar character less from its politics or religion, than from its industry. The application of steam and electricity to industry,

* Liberty-p.7. (Alden's Edition.)
+ Thomas Carlyle.
§ Herbert Spencer-Social Statics- p. 24 (Appelton's Edition.)

the wonderful succession of mechanical inventions with the
"large" system of production, the quickening and cheapening
of transportation and communication, the multiplication of
population, the anti-slavery agitation, the combinations and
conflicts of the new industrial classes, the yet new science
of political economy,-in brief-the Industrial Revolution,-
makes ours peculiarly the Industrial Age.

The Socialists seem to have been the first to recognize
most clearly the relation between the Zeit-Geist and the
struggle for liberty. "We must first of all notice that socialists have a somewhat different conception of liberty from
that which usually obtains. They have their minds fixed upon economic liberty, rather than political liberty. They
perceive that the chief restrictions upon freedom of movement
at the present time are economic in nature, and in this they
are quite correct. Any one who will reflect upon the things
which he desires to do, and upon those restrictions which keep
him from acting in accordance with those desires, will soon
discover that the restrictions upon his movements rarely proceed from government, but generally have their origin in lack
of resources. Restrictions proceed from lack of economic resources, and compulsion is connected with our economic necessities."* May it not, then, properly be said that industrial
liberty is the supreme guest and hope of the times?

* R.T.Ely- Socialism and Social Reform- pp. 207. 208

We therefore propose the following thesis for our present discussion, by way of both proof and illustration.

The best state of industrial liberty will exist in that condition of society which, by means both of private and collective effort, secures to its constituent members equality ofopportunity in their industrial interests.

This thesis will be developed by a series of inquiries concerning the following subjects:

I. The Nature of Industrial Liberty.

II. The Possibility of Industrial Liberty.

III. The Greatest Industrial Liberty.

IV. The Best Industrial Liberty.

V. Theories of Social Organization as Related to Industrial Liberty.
VI. Specific Measures as Related to Industrial Liberty.

I. The Nature of Industrial Liberty.

First question, what is industrial liberty?

This requires two subordinate inquiries.

1st, What is liberty in itself?

2nd, What is the relation of industry to liberty?

1st, What is liberty in itself?

An error at this point will obviously be misleading to our entire discussion, while an omission would leave us like an army cut off from its base of supplies. We will, therefore,

try to proceed safely by beginning with the narrowest possible conception of liberty and then feeling our way to the widest admissable conception.

1. <u>The narrowest possible conception of liberty is freedom from absolute co-ercion</u>.

For instance, one is under absolute compulsion to breathe with the lungs instead of the heart. Again, the enemies of the Bourbon Kings, arrested by lettres de cache and immured in the Bastile were absolutely co-erced to remain there at the King's pleasure. Of these two illustrations of restraint, we note that the first was both absolute and inevitable and admitted of no possible liberty from its limitations, while the second, though absolute, was both avoidable and remediable. We also note that the first belongs to the more usual class of absolute restraints (those proceeding from the laws of nature), and that the second belongs to a far less numerous class and is conditioned upon human agency. It is only with the second class that any theory of liberty can be concerned. Does a true concept of liberty include anything more than the removal of absolute restraints of this class? A few illustrations will show that the connotation of this word further embraces-

2. <u>Immunity from influences and hindrances unfavorable to desirable choices and actions</u>.

Observe that the word "desirable" is used, and not "desired". Mill says that "Liberty consists in doing what one desires."* But this will not prove an exact definition; for Mr. Mill himself tells us that a madman or an ignorant man may desire not to be free and freedom certainly does not consist in being free not to be free.+ Therefore, we say "desirable", not "desired". Of course the ultimate standard of desirability is a problem of ethics rather than of economics, and so need not detain us here.

In this part of our subject, illustration will have the force of proof. We are seeking to discover the accepted meaning of a word, and a mere inspection of instances will suffice to disclose whether or not they and the class to which they belong, are within that meaning. Liberty includes immunity from both restraining hindrances and restraining influences. We consider first,

(a) Hindrances- The difference between hindrances and absolute co-ercion as infringements of liberty may be exhibited by the following illustration. To be chained to a prison wall is an absolute privation of freedom of locomotion. To be chained to a cannon-ball, though only a hindrance to

---

* See D.G. Ritchie-Principles of State Interference, p. 86.
+ See Liberty, p. 172. (Alden's Edition).

freedom of locomotion and not its utter privation, is none
the less a real impairment thereof, and to break this chain
as well as to break the other would be a distinct contribution
to liberty.   In the words of J.M.Bonham: "The citizen in a
free state must be able to feel that he can embark in industrial enterprises without meeting all about him secret conditions which interrupt that right.   It is the duty of the
state to remove obstacles from the individual, so that he may
begin as well as prosecute his industries freely.   There must
be a power, therefore, which of its own motion will remove
insidious obstructions, and not delay the action until specific mischiefs are accomplished."*

    We will next illustrate,

    (b) Influences to undesirable choices and actions.

    (1) For example, if the victim of the lettre de cache
be excused from imprisonment if willing to suffer the amputa-
tion of his right hand, the compulsion put upon him is no
longer absolute since he can escape from it if willing to take
the consequences, but no one will argue that his liberty is
not really impaired by such duress.   Indeed, such is the familiar doctrine of municipal law.+

    (2)- Another illustration is given by Professor Huxley

---

* Industrial Liberty. p. 174.
+ See Blackstone-Commentaries,I, p. 131, 136, and II, p. 292.

showing that slavery itself has the character not of absolute but of moral co-ercion.

"It may seem a paradox to say that a slave-holder does not make his slaves work by force, but by agreement. And yet it is true. There is a contract between the two, which, if it were written out, would run in these terms: ' I undertake to feed, clothe, house, and not to kill, flog, or otherwise maltreat you, Quashie, if you perform a certain amount of work.' Quashie, seeing no better terms to be had, accepts the bargain, and goes to work accordingly."*

(3) Another illustration by Professor Huxley: "A high-wayman who garrotes me, and then clears out my pockets, robs me by force in the strict sense of the word; but if he puts a pistol to my head and demands my money or my life, and I preferring the latter, hand over my purse, we have virtually made a contract, and I perform one of the terms of the con-tract."+ This is none the less an infringement of the liberty of the one robbed.

Concerning the last three illustrations, there can be no dispute that they describe actual impairments of liberty. We will now cite two more illustrations which seem to be pre-cisely parallel to the three foregoing, and yet have not al-

* Administrative Nihilism-p. 47(Humboldt Paper Edition.)
+ Do.

ways been regarded as violations of liberty. They are further-
er significant as illustrating the incompleteness of political, apart from economic, liberty.

(4) Two men, an employer and a workingman, are making
a contract. The employer has more wealth than he needs for
his own comforts and luxuries; the workingman less than he
needs for his necessities. The workingman, who can get no
better terms elsewhere, must take what the employer offers
or starve. Clearly he is deprived of his liberty in the
same sense that the slave was; either one can accept the
terms or suffer the consequences. "Hunger is a good substi-
tute for the lash."*

(5) Mr. W.D.Howells shows as follows how a man's political liberty may sometimes be rendered nugatory by industrial tyranny. He says, "He may have the right to speak
freely, print freely, pray freely, vote freely; but he cannot
manfully use his right, though warranted in it by the constitutions and statutes of all the states, if he is afraid another man may take away his means of livelihood for so doing."+

These illustrations sufficiently extend the meaning of
liberty from immunity against <u>absolute</u> co-ercion to immunity

* Rodbertus- See Bohm-Bawerk- Capital and Interest,-p. XVII
of Introduction.
+ The Forum, December, 1895, p. 407.

from the moral or qualified co-ercion of hindrances and limit-
ing influences.   Connotation of the term be made to reach any
farther? We believe it can.

3- Thus far we have considered liberty in a merely
negative sense of "being left to oneself,"*- of "being free
from restraint and violence from others."+   We believe that
it may be also viewed positively as the increment of opportunities and powers. "True liberty is not simply the permis-
sion but the power to act freely."§   Freedom is "self-deter-
mined action directed to the objects of reason." #   It is a
positive power of doing or enjoying something worth doing or
enjoying, and that, too, something that we do or enjoy in
common with others." ‡

This analysis of the concept of liberty affords us the
elements for its synthesis.   We now have this definition:

Liberty, considered negatively is immunity from absolute co-ercion and from hindrances and influences unfavorable
to desirable choices and actions;   considered positively, it
is the increment of personal opportunities and powers.

---

* J.S.Mill-Liberty.
+ John Locke- Treatise of Government- Book II,Ch. VI, Sec. 57.
§ R.T.Ely,- Outlines of Economics, p. 42.
# See D.G.Ritchie- Principles of State Interference, p. 147.
‡ T.H.Green- Works- Vol. 3, p. 371.

2nd. What is the relation of industry to liberty?
The relation is two-fold.

1. Direct. Industry is related to liberty through
the influence of industrial phenomena upon the general freedom of individuals. For example, unduly long hours of labor
impair the health of the laborer and reduce his liberty by
diminishing his physical powers.

2. Indirect. Industry is indirectly related to liberty through such influences of the non-industrial phenomena
of society upon the industrial relations of individuals as
will affect their liberty. For example, popular education
is primarily a non-industrial institution, but by developing
the mental powers of individuals it increases their industrial
efficiency and thus augments their liberty.

The problem of industrial liberty, therefore, is concerned with all those social phenomena which condition human
freedom in or through the industrial relations of men.

II. The Possibility of Industrial Liberty.

Second question: In what sense is industrial liberty
possible?

This question resolves itself into two:

1st, Is absolute liberty possible? We can answer brief-
ly, No. Man is every where circumscribed by the laws of na-

ture and of his own being. Whatever freedom he may have must
be entirely within the inflexible limits set by these laws.

2nd. Is any liberty whatever possible to man?

Suffice it to say, that if there be any such thing as
liberty, it cannot be a property of material nature or the
physical constitution of man, since these are admittedly under
the dominance of iron necessity. It must be found, if found
at all, in the human soul. Therefore any system of philosophical determinism will cut short the development of any
theory of liberty at this point. Hence, in order to proceed
further in this discussion, we must either prove or assume
the doctrine of libertarianism. In this case proof would
require a long digression into the most difficult theories of
metaphysics, and as we are now treating an economic, not a
philosophical problem, we must be content with assumption.

How any necessitarian like Herbert Spencer, can frame
theories of liberty is hard to understand. Such a theory
would be only a theory about a nonentity, and the great necessitarian philospher is certainly estopped by his own words
from entering the lists as the Knight-errant of freedom. If
determinism be true, there is no such thing as liberty at all,
and government needs no more to promote it than to promote
the squaring of the circle . To free a man from political re-

straints would only give him over to other restraints which those political had shut off. According to the law of con-cervation of energy, a motive would then always be a motor; if free from some social co-ercion, he would be irresistably swayed by some cerebral co-ercion. There could then be no question of freedom, but only a question as to which of sev-eral equal restraints were more wholesome. There could be no dread of "the coming slavery", because absolute slavery had already come. To diminish or increase it would be im-possible; to alter its form the only possibility.

Let us further bear in mind that in its last analysis all seeming liberty that fails to give men a larger power of effectual moral choice, is actual tyranny, and that all seem-ing tyranny that eventuates in greater effectual freedom to the mind is actual liberty.

We, therefore, conclude,

1st, That liberty is possible only on the assumption of volitional freedom.

2nd, That industrial liberty may be promoted by such dispositions of industrial forces as shall conduce to the least restricted action and the highest development of the human will.

III. The Greatest Industrial Liberty.

Third question—In what would the highest degree of indus-

trial liberty consist?

We will enumerate and examine four theories propounded in answer to this question,--namely, the theories of Anarchy, Laissez-faire, Independence, and Equal Interdependence.

1st, The Theory of Anarchy.

This theory is that law per se is restriction and nothing else, and therefore that every law abolished leaves man by so much more free to determine his own acts.   The objection to this theory is that it also proposes to leave every man free to determine the acts of other men if he is wicked and strong or cunning enough to do so, and this comes as near as possible to destroying liberty altogether.   The following words of W.D. Howells are forcible and true: "Liberty is never a good in itself and is never final; it is a means to something good, and a way to the end which its lovers are seeking.   It is provisionally a blessing, but it is purely provisional; it is self-limited, and is forever merging into some sort of subjection. It no sooner establishes itself than it begins to control itself.   The dream of infinite and immutable liberty is the hallucination of the Anarchist, that is, of the Individualist gone mad.   The moment liberty in this meaning was achieved, we should have the rule, not of the wisest, not of the best, not even of the most, but of the

strongest, and no liberty at all."＊

To this the words of Professor Burgess may well be added: "Deprive the state, either wholly or in part, of the power to determine the elements and scope of individual liberty, and the result must be that each individual will make such determination, wholly or in part, for himself; that the determinations of different individuals will come into conflict with each other; and that those individuals only who have power to help themselves will remain free, reducing the rest to personal subjection."+

2nd. <u>The Theory of Laissez-Faire</u>.

This theory maintains, in common with Anarchism, that "restraint qua restraint is an evil,"§ and therefore that the only restraint admissable is that which restrains men from trespassing upon one another by violence, fraud or stealth. This theory belongs peculiarly to the "orthodox" political economy, and has its ablest support at present from Mr. Herbert Spencer.

Against this theory it may be charged:

1. That in practice it is bound to result in self-contradiction.

2. That it fails to guarantee the largest possible immunity from those forms of co-ercion exerted otherwise than

+ Political Science and Constitutional Law, vol. I,p.66.
§ J.S.Mill- Liberty, Chapter V.
＊ The Forum, December 1895, p. 403.

by one's fellow-men.

1,- Laissez-faire is inadequate as a theory of industrial liberty because of its practical inconsistencies.

This theory professes to stand midway between anarchy
and " State-interference". The logic of position involves
the two-fold inconsistency of requiring it at once to go back
to anarchism and advance to greater State-action.

a. Consistency would require the advocate of laissez-
faire to retreat to anarchism pure and simple.

Mr. Spencer grounds his doctrine of non-restriction in
the principle of natural selection. The struggle for existence is eliminating the unfit members of the race; therefore
let not the State interfere with this stern beneficence; interference would only make it easier for the unfit to survive at the expense of the fit. Nevertheless, Mr. Spencer
would say, let the State see that this process of selection
be free from violence or fraud.

But why without violence or fraud? In the animal
world at least, aggression and deceit are about all the methods
employed in the selective process, and Mr. Spencer himself has
said that "the poverty of the incapable, the distresses that
come upon the imprudent, the starvation of the idle, and those
shoulderings aside of the weak by the strong, which leave so

many in shallows and in miseries, are decrees of a large far-
seeing benevolence."*

Why then not trust this "large, far-seeing benevolence"
to the uttermost and allow men to shoulder each other aside
as much as they are strong or cunning enough to do, using all
the force or fraud they choose, since only the incapable would
thus be shouldered out of existence, while the capable survive to perpetuate a strong and ever stronger stock?   This
would be the logical inquiry of the Anarchist, and so far as
I know Mr. Spencer has failed to give a satisfactory answer.

b.   Consistency would otherwise require the advocate
of laissez-faire to concede a larger sphere than he does to
the activity of the State.

This theory permits State-interference to remedy violence or breach of contract in order that men may not in-
fringe each other's equal freedom.   But it is quite over-
looked that there may be just as much infringement of liberty
in the making of a contract (see infra. pp. 12 and 13) as in
its breach.   "The freedom to take the job or 'git' is the
cruellest of satires on liberty."+

* Social Statics, p. 322 (Edition of 1851.)
  See also "The Suis of Legislators" in The Man vs. the State.
+ The twentieth Century, N.Y. April 2, 1891.

Says Professor Huxley: "Suppose, however, for the sake
of argument, that the functions of the State may be properly
summed up in the one great negative commandment "Thou shalt
not allow any man to interfere with the liberty of any other
man'- I am unable to see that the logical consequence is any
such restriction of the power of government, as its suppor-
ters imply. If my next door neighbour chooses to have his
drains in such a state as to create a poisonous atmosphere
which I breathe at the risk of typhus and diphtheria, he re-
stricts my just freedom to live just as much as if he went
about with a pistol, threatening my life; if he is to be allowed to let his children go unvaccinated, he might as well
be allowed to leave strychnine-lozenges in the way of mine;
and if he brings them up untaught and untrained to earn their
living, he is doing his best to restrict my freedom, by in-
creasing the burden of taxation, for the support of jails and
workhouses, which I have to pay. The higher the state of
civilization, the more completely do the actions of one member
of the social body influence all the rest, and the less possible is it for any one man to do a wrong thing without interfering, more or less, with the freedom of all his fellow
citizens. So that even upon the narrowest view of the functions of the State, it must be admitted to have wider powers

than the advocates of the police-theory are willing to admit."*

    2.   Laissez-faire also leaves out of account all the non-social restraints under which man labours.

    These are of two sorts.

    a.   Those of personal character.

    b.   Those of natural environment.

    While as has been said (see pp. 16 and 17 infra) the laws governing these restraints cannot be made to yield, yet the conditions upon which these laws operate can be so altered as to promote the volitional freedom of the individual. We consider first

    a- The restraints of personal character.

    If it be true, as Mr. Spencer says, that "whatever amount of power an organism expends in any shape is the correlate and equivalent of a power that was taken into it from without,"+ then it must follow that it is necessary to the fullest liberty of the individual that some of the dispositions of his own nature which came into him from outside without his own choice, must be restrained. For instance, a disposition to sensual indulgences may, if itself unrestrained, place him under numerous restraints; may, for instance, so burden him with poverty or disease as to reduce his liberty

* Administrative Nihilism, pp. 41 and 42. (Humboldt's Edition.)
+ Principles of Biology, p. 57.

to almost a nullity.   In such a case the less liberty of one
kind should be taken away in order to secure the greater liberty of another kind. Laissez-faire would fail to even attempt his protection from self-oppression.

b.- Laissez-faire also fails to take account of the
tyranny of environment.

For instance, a miasmatic swamp lies near a village;
its presence is a constant menace to the liberty of the villagers, even their liberty to live. Nevertheless, there is
not wealth or skill enough in the village to drain the swamp.
The villagers appeal to the State for aid. Laissez-faire
would say, "In the name of Liberty let the State keep hands
off".   And the tyranny of environment would go on.

We believe it thus established that if we seek the
largest industrial liberty in laissez-faire (the minimum of
political activity) we are on the one hand led by the logic
of our position to anarchy (in which liberty includes liberty
to oppress) or on the other hand, are compelled to submit to
numberless non-political restraints, some social, some non-
social, but many of them of the most oppressive character.

3rd.   The Theory of Independence.

This theory regards the largest industrial liberty as
possible only in that social state where every individual was

wholly independent of every other in industrial affairs. Arnold Toynbee would seem to represent this theory. In a passage in his essay on "Ricardo and the Old Political Economy",
setting forth the futility of liberty without economic independence,* this theory is at least implicit.

This theory comes near the truth, but fairly misses it.
Independence in its exact sense is impossible in civilized
society. The theory is an ill-timed reminiscence of Rousseau's encomiums upon savagery. Says Prof. Gunton: "We should
be careful not to confound freedom with independence. The
savage is independent of social restrictions, but he has very
little freedom. He is in constant danger of his life from
the defenselessness of his position. He has no friends because he befriends nobody; he can obtain no assistance or
protection because he assists and protects nobody. Indeed
it is because he is the least dependent upon his fellows that
he is the most helpless and has the least freedom of any man
in the world."+

Indeed Prof. Gunton goes too far in asserting even the
savage to be strictly "independent of social restraints".
Ever since men have been gregarious animals, that is, since

---

* See A. Toynbee. "The Industrial Revolution." p. 17, (Humboldt's Edition.)
+ Principles of Social Economics, pp. 310, 311.

they began to be men at all, they must have been to some degree dependent upon one another, and the more civilized the
more dependent. The science of sociology derives its very
possibility of being from the truth that no man liveth or can
live to himself alone.

4th.- The Theory of Equal Interdependence.

The proposition is this: The greatest industrial liberty would exist when all men having industrial relations
with each other were equally dependent on one another within
those relations.   This theory seems true.

Observe that it is said "equally" dependent.   In case
of equal dependence neither of two men can be subject to any
hardship or oppression at the hands of the other.   The other,
being equally dependent upon the first, by attempting any aggression would only impair his own welfare to an equal degree.   Men would all, like the Siamese twins, be equally dependent for health and life upon each other.   In such a social state infringement of liberty could be prompted only by
madness.

Several suggestions of this theory might be cited.
Indeed it is possible that something like this is in the minds
of those who write inaptly of "economic independence".   Certainly Arnold Toynbee gives a hint of such a meaning when in

the passage referred to above, he writes approvingly, "of free
competition of equal industrial unites."*

Herbert Spencer portrays a similar state of society.
It will, however, be seen, I think that in the words I am a-
bout to quote, Mr. Spencer unconsciously fails to reconcile
his theory with any possibility of social progress.   In a
pamphlet on "The Classification of the Sciences" he says:
"The units of any aggregate of matter are in equilibrium when
they severally act and re—act upon each other on all sides
with equal forces.* * * * Similarly among the units of a
society, the fundamental condition of equilibrium is, that
the restraining forces which the units exercise on each other
shall be balanced.   If the spheres of action of some units
are diminished by extension of the spheres of action of others,
there necessarily results an unbalanced force which tends to
produce political change in the relations of individuals; and
the tendency to change can cease, only when individuals cease
to aggress on each other's spheres of action— only when there
is maintained that law of equal freedom which it was the purpose of 'Social Statics' to enforce in all its consequences."+
And in Social Statics, Mr. Spencer says: "Individuals, as u-

*"Ricards and the Old Political Economy," See Industrial
   Revolution, p. 17.
+ Quoted in Social Statics, p. X of Introductory Notice.
   (Appleton's Edition.)

nits of the social mass, tend to assume like relations with
the atoms of matter, surrounded as these are by their respective atmospheres of repulsion as well as of attraction.   And
perhaps social stability may ultimately be seen to depend upon the due balance of these forces."*

A passage from Professor Gunton's Social Economics con-
tains a similar suggestion.   He says: "Mutual dependence is.
the great promoter of freedom.   Whenever the freedom of each
depends upon the freedom of all, no one has any interest in
preventing it.   Mutual dependence cancels obligation and
extends freedom, while dependence creates obligation and re-
stricts freedom.   It is only when every body's safety depends upon protecting the safety of his neighbor that freedom extends along the whole line of human relations. * * * It
is only the mutual assistance born of individual interdependence that can make the highest social life and the maximum individual freedom possible."+

Industrial liberty, then, is most highly afforded, not
in anarchy, which would be the negation of liberty, nor in
laissez-faire, which is only anarchy minus part of its unre-
strained aggression, nor in independence, which is contrary
to the nature of society, but in equal interdependence.

* p. 111.
+ p. 311.

24

IV. <u>The Best Industrial Liberty</u>.

Fourth question: Supposing a state of equal interdependence to exist perfectly we ask, would it be the best possible social state?   And if not, to what extent could such
interdependence be extended consistently with the best interests of society.

1st. Is absolutely equal interdependence the best
possible social state?

The existing inequalities among men are the reason why
their reciprocal dependence upon each other is unequal. These
inequalities are of two sorts. First, those due solely to
personal endowments. Second, those resulting from the acci-
dent of environment.

There are two possible ways whereby such inequalities
between individuals could be prevented from working oppression.
One way is by such a moral regeneration of the stronger, such
a cultivation of his altruism, that he will take no oppressive
advantages of his superiority.   The other way is to destroy
the inequalities. This cannot, of course, be accomplished
by robbing men of those superior endowments which are parts
of their own being.   Nor would such a measure be desirable
if possible; gifted men are not too plentiful.

In two other ways these inequalities might conceivably

be overcome.

First, by a process of culture afforded to the inferior man and designed to train him up to equality with the man of endowments. But this, in order to be effectual would involve withholding culture from the superior man and is of course out of the question. Nor would it be practicable.

The other method would be so to re-distribute the inequalities of environment as to exactly conpensate the inequalities of endowment. Suppose A to have natural faculties which may be represented quantitatively by 10x and advantages in his circumstances which may be represented by 8x; total 18x. Suppose B to have endowments indicated by 5x and favorable circumstances indicated by 3x; total 8x. To render their mutual dependence equal it will be necessary to deprive A of circumstantial advantages equal to 5x and confer them upon B. Their respective abilities will then be,

A $(10 + 8 - 5)x = 13x$

B $(5 + 3 + 5)x = 13x,$

and their interdependence equal. Such a re-organization of society, if universal and permanent, would give the most liberty possible. Would it give the best liberty?

It certainly would not. It has been said sometimes that liberty is a good in itself, but the proof has never been

forthcoming.   Liberty, as Mr. Howells said (see infra p. 20
and 21) is only provisionally good; good as a means to an
end.   A state of society in which all equality had been
brought about by taking the bulk of the wealth or other circumstantial advantages from the gifted and giving them to the
incapable would put both the gifted and the incapable into
such a position as to render either unable to domineer very
much over the other, but it would at the same time utterly
paralyze all incitement to individual effort, deprive society of the best service of its best servants and ultimately
drag down the whole race to the level of its least gifted members. It is in the dissimilar endowments of men that the possibilities of all individual development and all general progress inhere.

Not so the accidents of environment, such as family,
inherited wealth, residence, occupation, etc. (so far as these
are accidents).   These inequalities (not including, of course,
such as are consequent upon the exertions of natural faculties), should be abolished wherever possible.   They include
every hindrance to the highly endowed and worthy men and the
bulwarks of the inefficient and unworthy.   These "accidents"
are the improvidence that runs athwart the providence of natural selection to cause its enormous waste. (See infra,pp.

27

80-82). Just as truly as a vigorous young lion may starve
to death in a famine-stricken land, while a puny young lion,
finding himself in a place of plenty, may live to perpetuate
his kind, so truly may a man of the noblest capacity be thwart-
ed by untoward circumstances, while the effeminate child of
aristocracy rolls in unearned luxury, lays commands upon a
score of servants, and becomes the father of a generation of
imbeciles. Says Mr. Galton in his great work on **Hereditary
Genius**: "If the 'eminent men' of any period, had been change-
lings when babies, a very fair proportion of those who survive and retained their health up to fifty years of age, would,
notwithstanding their altered circumstances, have equally
risen to eminence. Thus- to take a strong case- it is in-
credible that any combination of circumstances, could have
repressed Lord Brougham to the level of undistinguished medi-
ocrity."* Upon this passage David G. Ritchie comments as
follows: "Mr. Galton's example is well chosen for his purpose.
Lord Bougham was just the kind of a man who would anywhere
have pushed himself into notoriety of some kind. But those
social hindrances 'which form a system of natural selection',
may allow a great many Lord Boughams to come to the front in
different disguises and yet may repress some one who might do

---

* p. 38.

the world more service than an indefinite array of Lord Boughams. Suppose Mr. Darwin had had to pass his life as an over-
worked and over-worried country surgeon, or had been a fac-
tory hand in a large manufacturing town, he might conceivably
have been a noted man in a small naturalist's club, and been
lauded by his neighbors for collecting beetles; but would
he have discovered the origin of species and proved his dis-
covery? It is perfectly true that'social hindrances cannot
impede men of high ability from eminence,' and that 'social
advantages are incompetent to give that status to a man of
moderate ability.' But'social hindrances' may exhaust all
the energy of the ablest in the bare struggle for existence,
and may direct the energy of those who do succeed into wrong
and mischievous channels. We cannot invent a machine for
manufacturing genius, but we might do something to eliminate
the waste and misapplication of genius that goes on at present".*

Says Professor Huxley: "We have all known noble lords
who would have been coachmen, or gamekeepers, or billiard-
markers, if they had not been kept afloat by our social corks;
we have all known men among the lowest ranks, of whom every
one has said: 'What might not that man have become if he had
only had a little education'. And who that attends, even in
the most superficial way, to the condition upon which the sta-

* Darwinism and Politics, pp. 24-25.

bility of modern society- and especially of a society like
ours, in which recent legislation has put sovereign power in
the hands of the masses, whenever they are united enough to
wield their power- can doubt that every man of high natural
ability, who is both ignorant and miserable, is as great a
danger to society as a rocket without a stick is to the people who fire it?   Misery is a match that never goes out;
genius, as an explosive power, beats gunpowder hollow; and
if knowledge, which should give that power guidance, is want-
ing, the chances are not small that the rocket will simply run
a-muck among friends and foes."*

The ideal industrial liberty, then, is not absolutely
equal interdependence, which could only result in an enervat-
ing repression of all individual incentive, but is that degree
of liberty which would afford to all members of society equal
opportunities to achieve that industrial position for which
their personal endowments and merits fit them.

V. Theories of Social Organization as
Related to Industrial Liberty.

Fifth question: What principle of social organization
will best promote equality of industrial opportunity?

---

* Administrative Nihilism, p. 39, (Humboldt Edition.)

30

Four theories will be considered:

    1st. Anarchy.

    2nd. Laissez-faire.

    3rd. State-Action.

    4th. Socialism.

1st. <u>Anarchy</u>.

Anarchy is society without the state. It might seem at first that the removal of legal sanctions would leave to institutions, privileges, and property no support except that given by the capability of individuals; in other words, that it would put to an equal test the personal endowments of each, giving artificial aid or hindrance to no one. There would be three respects, however, in which anarchy would fail to attain this ideal.

1. It would fail to promote liberty in the positive sense.

For **instance**, supposing educational institutions even possible under anarchy, a child with good natural endowments, but having ignorant or otherwise incapable parents would have no opportunity for proper development of his powers without public provision for his education.

2. It would fail to give individuals the highest possible security against accidents of nature.

31

It is hard to see, for instance, how an effectual quarantine system could be operated without the agency of the State.

3. It would fail to give proper incentive to the exercise of any endowments except physical strength and aggressive cunning. Diligence, frugality, inventiveness, etc., would be at a discount of one hundred per cent when the double possibility were everywhere imminent, of losing all or gaining as much by violence or treachery.

Opposed to each other as the chief social theories are Laissez-faire and State-Action. We will, therefore, consider them largely in comparison.

2nd. Laissez-Faire.

This theory may be set forth in the following series of propositions:

1. Greatest happiness is the supreme good, but owing to its indefiniteness, not the immediate test of social conduct and legislation.*

2. Happiness is to be secured to the individual only by leaving every man free to exercise his own faculties as he will.+

3. "Wherefore we arrive at the general proposition

---

* See H. Spencer-Social Statics, Introduction, sec. 1-5. Also J.S. Mill, Utilitarianism, p. 55, note, (Humboldt Edition.)
+See H. Spencer, Social Statics, Ch. IV, sec. 2.

that every man may claim the fullest liberty to exercise his
facultiescompatible with the possession of like liberty by
every other man."*

    4.   Therefore the only functions of the State are its
police-functions-protection of individuals from the aggres-
sions-violent, stealthy, or fraudulent,-of one another.+

    5.   Beyond this limit all state activity is unwarrant-
able- (a) because an infringement of equal freedom-(b) because
it could not be intelligently performed.

    6.   Within this limit social progress is insured by
the principle of natural selection.

    The test of this theory is to be its fitness to secure
to the members of society equality of industrial opportunity.
Bearing this test in mind, the following criticisms of laissez-faire seem to be valid.

    1.   It is self-contradictory(see infra pp. 23-28).

    2. It fails in that the best it professes to offer
comes too late for the period of greatest need. The most
stubborn and fatal inequalities of opportunity establish themselves during the period of personal immaturity, forestall-
ing the development of those endowments which might, at a la-
ter period, have overcome them, Among such inequalities are
the following.

---

* Do. Chapter IV. Section 3.
+ Do. Chapters XXI and XXII.

a. **Heredity.** Of course the State cannot influence the heredity of one already born, but by better protecting the childhood of one generation from unwholesome environments it will insure a better heredity to the next.

b. **Rosidonce.** To be brought up in an over-crowded tenement is almost sure to stunt the development of body and mind. Tenement children brought up in tenements usually become brutish or unhealthy. Tenement children removed to farms usually grow up to as great efficiency as those born there.

c. **Education.** The industrial efficiency of the man will depend on the training of his childhood. Ignorance will be a permanent limitation of his industrial liberty.

d. **Inheritance.** Suppose the millionaire's son and the pauper's son to have equal endowments and education. The one begins business with a million dollars of capital, the other with no capital. Their respective opportunities of success are almost as unequal as their fortunes.

It has not been contended here that these inequalities thus determined in childhood could be all remedied at once and completely by any measures now known to society and waiting to be applied, but only that if there be remedies, they are obviously to consist in something else than leaving things as they are.

34

3.   The principle of laissez-faire overlooks the quasi-public character of some of those institutions which most effectually restrict industrial liberty.

The corporation is the creature of the State. Laissez-faire at one time might have said, "Let no such creature be called into being". But that time has gone by. The corporation has come to stay. It has acquired some of the attributes of the political sovereign, and industrial power such as no natural person could ever acquire, until whole communities and whole industries are firm in its relentless grasp.*   The story of monopolies and trusts at once withholding from their employes' and exacting from their customers fabulous sums of wealth— of railroads and their "parasites" ruining competitors and oppressing the public,- are all too familiar.   These creatures of the State can defy competition and use it as their own instrument of oppression.   The power that created them is the only power that can curb their encroachments.+

4. Laissez-laire fails to secure equality of opportunity in that accidents of the market which cannot be foreseen impoverish one and enrich another, both of whom had equal endowments and had made equal sacrifices for the common good.

* See J.M.Bonham – Industrial Liberty- pp. 113 and 128.
+ See J.M.Bonham- Industrial Liberty- Chapters III, IV, & V.

35

Three opportunities are necessary to the industrial
liberty of producers. (a) Opportunity to produce. (b) Opportunity to seek buyers. (c) Opportunity to find buyers.
Admitting that laissez-faire would afford the first two opportunities, the third opportunity is left entirely dependent
upon contingencies which can be but vaguely anticipated by
most producers,- namely upon the accidents of supply and demand.

"How is what one gets determined (under the present
system)? Not really by the utility of what one produces and
has to sell, not either by the cost of producing it and bringing it to market; but rather by the quantity of things of
the same sort that happen to be in the market. If there is
much of it, buyers can take advantage of the producer, and
give little ; if there is little, the producer can take advantage of those who wish to buy, and get much. Such is the
working and meaning of the so-called law of supply and demand."*

Mr. Spencer defines justice as "a rigorous maintenance
of those normal relations among citizens in which each gets
in return for his labor, skilled or unskilled, bodily or mental, as much as is proved to be its worth by the demand for
it; such return therefore as will enable him to thrive and
rear offspring, in proportion to the superiorities which make

* W.M.Salter, Anarchy of Government, p. 105.

him valuable to himself and others."* By comparing the two
clauses of the above sentence, we have the plain proposition
that the (almost constant) industrial superiorities of a producer are exactly measured by the (always fluctuating) demand-
value of his services. This proposition is not only mathe-
matically absurd, but it is contradicted by facts familiar
to every body. We have all seen men with excellent powers
of body and mind bring into the market a commodity of which
there had occurred an unforeseen abundance, and perhaps meet
bankruptcy, while some very inferior man had brought to market a commodity of which there was an unforeseen scarcity, and
achieved his fortune. Again, we have seen admirably gifted
and trained for some single vocation, and yet because that
vocation has become over-crowded, compelled to employ their
admirable powers with but little profit either to themselves
or to society, while other men though poorly gifted and trained for another vocation, are yet prosperous therein simply because they have few competitors. It may be said that the
law of supply and demand will in such a case deplete the ranks
of the one vocation and recruit those of the other. True;
but in the case of skilled occupations at least, this cannot
be fully achieved until another generation has received an ad-

---

* The Man vs. The State, p. 86.
See also Mr. Spencer's "Rejoinder to M. de Laveleye,"
Contemporary Review, April, 1895.

equate training. And by that time the waste and hardship and
end of opportunity will be past prevention, while the new
generation will be apt to go in the very opposite extreme.

Again, we have not been contending that State intervention has ready at hand a known remedy for these inequalities, but that if there be a remedy for them it must be something other than the "hands-off" policy. It is the very essence of the meaning of laissez-faire to attempt no remedy
here; indeed, it refuses to recognize any ill calling for
correction. Mr. Spencer regards it as the only industrial
function of government to give the widest possible sway to
the law of supply and demand. * "Interference with the law
of supply and demand" he writes large among "the sins of legislators." And Professor W.G.Sumner declares that the distribution which takes place under the law of supply and demand gives us the only definition of justice which can be
seriously considered.+

Compared with these views, the rival theory has the
merit of at least recognizing the inequality and seeking a
remedy. Here is the important problem which laissez-faire
refuses to recognize as any problem at all: How shall such

* Sociology, Vol. II, sections 587, 588.
  "The Sins of Legislators", in The Man vs.the State.
+ Princeton Review, November, 1882.

a co-ordination of supply and demand be secured as to give to
each the opportunity of exercising his best faculties to the
mutual profit of himself and society?

A suggestion of a partial answer is given by John
Stuart Mill: "What the State can usefully do is to make itself a central depository, and active circulator and diffuser
of experience resulting from many trials."*

5. Laissez-faire makes certain false assumptions.

a.- It is falsely assumed that the only co-ercion to
be averted is political co-ercion.

This assumption is implied in the very title of Mr.
Spencer's work The Man vs. the State, and in the titles of its
four chapters, The New Toryism, The Coming Slavery, The Sins
of Legislators, and The Great Political Superstition. Indeed
it is true of all his political writings and of all the writings of his school, that their every plea for liberty is simply a plea for less legislation.+

Liberty consists not in the absence of laws, but in the
character of the laws. There are, as we have seen many sorts
of liberty and these are all closely dependent upon each o-
ther. They interact. Government has, then, this function
or none at all: to curtail certain liberties for the purpose

---

*Liberty, p. 184 (Alden's Edition). See also do. p. 190, and
 J.S.Mill Political Economy, Book V, Chapter XI, section 1.
+ See the closing paragraph of The Man vs. the State.

of protecting or promoting greater liberties. This is anal-
ogous to the principle of mechanics, that the greatest effectual power is secured, not by the removal of all control,
but by intelligently controlling its exertion. Every man is
bound by a thousand fetters not forged by the State. It is
the business of the State to break these fetters. Where social, economic, or physical laws bind a man, the State should
give him liberty if possible. "There are matters in which
the interference of law is required, not to over-rule the
judgment of individuals respecting their own interests, but
to give effect to that judgment, they being unable to give
effect to it except by concert, which concert again cannot be
effectual unless it receives validity and sanction from the
law. For illustration, and without prejudging the particular point, I may advert to the question of diminishing the
hours of labor."*

Further illustrations may be added. For example, the
vast majority desire to rest one day in seven, but the uncon-
trolled economic law of competition would deprive them of
this liberty. The State here adds to the aggregate liberty
by thwarting the operation of this economic law; i.e. by for-
bidding all competitors to work on one day in the week. Again,
a man's physical powers are broken by disease. He is thereby

* J.S.Mill, Political Economy, Book V, Chap. XI, sec. II.

restrained from doing a thousand things he desires to do.
His liberty is greatly curtailed by natural law. Further, he
communicates the disease to several others, and their liberty
also becomes impaired. If municipal law had curtailed his
liberty to the slight degree of compelling him to be vaccinat-
ed, it would have saved in the end an incomparably greater a-
mount of liberty than it sacrificed.

By way of further illustration I quote from Professor
Ritchie's work on The Principles of State Interference. "In
what we call 'society' there are many associations or communities besides the great community which we call the State.
There is the family (both in the sense of familia or household, and in the sense of gens or clan); there are all the
various professions and trades, whether explicitly organized
in guilds or unions or not; there are all churches and religious bodies; there are ancient and powerful corporations,
with charters and privileges and customary rights; there are
also modern and powerful joint-stock companies; and there
are all the various combinations between man and man formed
by contracts of all sorts. The head of the household, if left
to himself to act, 'like the Cyclops' in patriarchal manner,
might exer ise his patria polestas in a way which would interfere with the just liberty— i.e. what we are coming to regard

as the just liberty- of wife, children, and servants. The
State steps in to protect them by direct legislation, or by
sanctioning legal remedies against the exercise of customary
privileges with which in the good old days it would never
have dared to meddle, or dreamt of meddling. The trades
guilds exercised an authority over individuals to which the
State has gradually put an end. The State has restrained religious bodies from exercising the control they wished over
the opinions and conduct of individuals. We arebeginning to
find out that the powers of gas and water companies, and the
relations between landlord and tenant, between employer and
employed, nay, even between parent and child, frequently need
State interference in the interests of individual freedom."*

     The following words of Professor Jevons may also be
quoted in this connection : "The modern English citizen who
lives under the burden of the revised edition of the Statutes,
not to speak of municipal, railroad, sanitary, and other by-
laws, is, after all, an infinitely freer as well as nobler
creature than the savage who is always under the despotism of
physical want."+

     Therefore to liberate is not to minimize municipal laws,
but to make it possible for society to so correlate municipal

---

* pp. 92 and 93.
+ The State in Relation to Labor, pp. 14, 15.

to other laws as to diminish the limitations which these laws
have placed upon human opportunities. Political liberty is
desirable only so far as it contributes to the best general
liberty of society. We buy the greater by selling the less
liberty. The ideal political liberty is that adjustment of
legislation which gives to the individual the freest scope
for the development of his highest aptitudes. Its test is
not quantity but quality. Its aim would be to protect each
from his neighbor and all from their environments; in short,
to make it as easy as possible for men to seek their interests untrammeled by circumstances beyond control of individual action but within control of collective action. Tyranny
is found in a thousand forms other than legislative co-ercion,
and liberty in a thousand forms other than thin statute-books.

b.- Laissez-faire falsely assumes "that all power gained by the State is so much taken from the individual; and, con-
versely that all power gained by the individual is gained at
the expense of the State."*

This assumption underlies Mill on <u>Liberty</u> and Spencer's
<u>The Man vs. the State</u>. Now Mr. Spencer himself unwittingly
conducts us to two different standpoints whence we can clearly discern the emptiness of this important assumption.

* D.G. Ritchie- Principles of State Interference, p. 12.

43

(1) In the first place, Mr. Spencer has likened society to an animal organism, the legislative authority of one
corresponding to the cerebral masses of the other.* This pre-
pares us for the following interesting process of inference.

(a) All power gained by the State is taken from the
individual.

(b) The State is related to society as the brain to
the body.

Conclusion: Therefore all increase of brain-power correspondingly decreases the power of all the rest of the body.

Either Mr. Spencer is incorrect in regarding society
as such an organism, or else it is possible for government
and the individual to gain power together.

(2) Again, Mr. Spencer often states that the indivu-
al is freer under the modern than under the mediaeval state.+
Is this because the mediaeval state had greater power than
the modern? Exactly the opposite is true. In the words of
Sir J. Fitzjames Stephen: "The difference between a rough and
a civilized society is not that force is used in the one case
and persuasion in the other, but that force is (or ought to
be) guided with greater care in the second case than in the

* D.G.Ritchie--Principles of State Interference, p. 20.
+ See for instance, "The New Toryism" in The Man vs. the State.

first.   President Lincoln attained his objects by the use
of a degree of force which would have crushed Charlemagne and
his paladins like egg-shells."*   It is, then, hardly a matter of dispute that the powers of states and the freedom of
individuals have been growing together.

C.- A kindred assumption equally false is that physical force applied is the only form of co-ercion to be regarded.

In the growing tendency to apply political remedies to
industrial maladies Mr. Spencer finds the very essence of
Toryism, which originated in militancy and stands for compulsory co-operation. +   This assumes that because force is
the ultimate sanction of political authority, no other co-
ercion is involved in the phenomena concerned.

The fact is that physical force is a comparatively
small factor in the problem of liberty.   For example, a
drunkard begets a child; the child is born an embodiment of
evil passions; the future of the child is thus largely determined for evil by the parent. That child is not only himself a slave, but likewise a menace to society. If by law
his father's liberty to become intoxicated had been curtailed,
the child would have been free from a law which curtails his

* Liberty, Equality, Fraternity, p. 32 (2nd Edition).
+ "The New Toryism", in The Man vs. the State.

freedom far more than the State need have restrained that of
his father.

d. and e.- The next two wrong assumptions of this theory
will be treated together with a third and true assumption.
We borrow the words of another. "This theory (laissez-faire)
derives its chief plausibility from a seeming universality in
its postulates which are : (1) That self-interest is a universal principle in human nature. (2) That each individual knows
his own interest best, and in the absence of arbitrary restrictions is sure to follow it. (3) That free competition always develops the highest possibilities by enabling each to
do that for which he is best fitted, and thereby most advance
the welfare of all. The proposition that self-interest is a
universal principle in human nature is undoubtedly correct,
but there is nothing in experience or logic to warrant the
assumption that the other two follow it."*

f.   The theory of laissez-faire wrongly assumes the
sufficiency of natural selection apart from the collective
action of society, to secure the social welfare and progress.+

(1) The first error of this assumption is another assumption which it involves- namely, the distinction between
collective social action and the selective forces of nature.

* G. Gunton- Principles of Social Economics, p. 286.
+ J.M.Bonham,-Industrial Liberty, p. 185.

46

"We commonly employ the term nature as if it represented only
the unconscious cosmic forces, as distinguished from conscious
human forces. And thus we speak of the products of human device as artificial, just as if human arrangements were unnat-
ural."* And Professor Ritchie writes as follows: "But the
difficulty is, where are we to find a line between 'natural
and artificial', if all the phenomena of society are, as the
evolutionist is bound to hold, subject to the same laws of -
nature? Now what does all this amount to except a recognition of the difference introduced into natural evolution by
the appearance of human consciousness?"+ Again the same writ-
er says: "Governments are natural products and it is inconsistent in Mr. Herbert Spencer, while telling us that the max-
im 'Constitutions are not made but grow' has become a truism,
to go on to blame governments because they interfere with natural laws. Why, such 'interferences' would on his own principles amount to a miracle! The real and significant distinction is not between 'State-interference' and 'laissez-faire',
but between intelligent and scientific, i.e., systematic and
far-sighted State-action on one side and that peddling kind

* G.Gunton- Principles of Social Economics, p. 288.
+ Darwinism and Politics, pp. 13 & 14 (Humboldt Edition).

of playing at an occasional and condescending providence in
small matters which is often much worse than doing nothing at
all." ⌐

Therefore it yet remains to be said why State-action
shall be denied a legitimate and natural place among the fac-
tors of evolution.

(2) Considered merely as "the struggle for existence"
natural selection fails to insure the survival of the (social-
ly) fittest."

That sociologists like Mr. Spencer consider natural
selection as practically synonomous with the struggle for
existence is implicit in almost everything they urge against
State action. The substance of all such strictures is that
State-action takes from the worthy for the benefit of the unworthy, thus hindering the former and aiding the latter to
thrive and propagate.+

Such evolutionists would do well to remember something
said by Darwin himself. "Important as the struggle for existence has been and still is," he wrote, "yet as far as the
highest part of man's nature is concerned, there are other
agencies more important"§

---

* Darwinism and Politics, p. 15 (Humboldt Edition).
+ See "Sins of Legislators", in The Man vs. the State.
§ The Descent of Man- p. 319.

48

Indeed the phrase "survival of the fittest," as commonly used, does not mean the survival of the fittest in every
sense, or even in the highest, the ethical sense but only as
Professor Huxley said, the survival of those "best fitted to
cope with their circumstances."* The fittest do not always
survive "except in the sense in which the proposition is a
truism, that those survive who are most capable of surviving."+
In May Kendall's rhyme the ichthyosaurus sings,

> "We dined, as a rule, on each other,
>
> What matter? The toughest survived."§

And so far as "the struggle for existence" is a factor in human, as in ichthyosaurus selection, it may as well be called
the survival of the <u>toughest</u> as the survival of the <u>fittest</u>.
"Among the lower animals physical strength or agility is the
favored quality; if some heaven-sent genius among the cuttle-
fish developed a delicate poetic faculty, this high excellence
would not delay his succumbing to his hulking neighbors."#

Human history abounds with instances of "high excel-
lence" thus succumbing to "toughness". Fox's <u>Book</u> <u>of</u> <u>Martyr's</u>
is a monument to the failure of the struggle for existence to preserve the
fittest. Almost every daily newspaper and every man's per-

---

* Article on "The Struggle for Existence" in the "Nineteenth
  Century, February, 1888, p. 165.
+ D.G.Ritchie- Darwinism and Politics, p. 10.
§ Dreams to Sell-"Ballad of the Ichthyosaurus".
# Sidney Webb in Fabian Essays.

sonal observation might be cited in evidence. For instance,
it is an every day occurrence for some unprincipled speculator
to make his life-fortune by one immoral trick, while thous-
ands of industrious and upright men are dragging out lives of
weariness and penury.*   This is neither "survival of the
fittest" nor "industrial liberty."

This failure of the struggle for existence as a system
of social therapentics is due in part to the counteracting
influences which it encounters in certain human institutions,
which institutions we may fairly assume to be beneficent and
necessary. In other words, in order to test natural selection
on its merits we must go back to the naked unsocialism of
nature.+   Among the modifying institutions referred to we
select a few by way of illustration.

(a) National organizations.

"We must emphasize the fact that the struggle goes on
not merely between individual and individual, but between race
and race. * * * * So soon as we pass to the struggle between
race and race, we find new elements coming in. The race which
is fittest to survive, i.e., most capable of surviving, will
survive; but it does not follow that the individuals thereby
preserved will be the fittest, either in the sense of being

---

* See Laveleye, "Review of The Man vs. the State." Contemporary Review.
+ See D.G.Ritchie-Darwinism and Politics,p. 13(Humboldt Edition).

those who in a struggle between individual and individual
would have survived, or in the sense of being those whom we
should regard as being the finest specimens of their kind.
A race or nation may succeed by crushing out the chances of
the great majority of its individual members.   The cruel pol-
ity of the bees, the slave-holding propensities of certain
ants have their analogues in human societies.   The success
of Sparta in the Hellenic world was obtained at the cost of
a frightful oppression of her subject classes, and with the
result that Sparta never produced one really great man. How
much more does the world really owe to Athens, which failed,
than to Sparta which succeeded in the physical struggle for
existence."*

(b) Marriage and the family.

Hereditary succession alone is often sufficient to a-
bolish the law of natural selection.(See infra p. 52.)   Mar-
riages are often determined by "society" qualifications rather than social qualifications (mutual fitness of the pair).
Hence deteriorated offspring.+

(c) Property.

The struggle for existence as carried on in the state
of nature may be illustrated as follows.   A sickly old lion
captures a gazelle; his stronger young brother deprives him

* D.G.Ritchie- Darwinish and Politics, p. 10 (Humboldt Edition)
+ See Laveleye-"Review of Man vs. the State" in Contemporary
  Review.

of the prey; the old lion starves; the younger one perpetu-
ates the stock.   But in a civilized society under the regeme
of property the physical struggle for existence would be likely to assume the following form.   The infirm old "speculator" amasses a fortune, marries and begets a family of puny
children; some young Hercules attempts to rob him of his
fortune; the law seizes Hercules and imprisons him; he dies
a convict, and "natural" selection is here entirely supersed-
ed by what would be called the "artificial" selection of the
law.*

In view of all these considerations we believe that
John Fiske is warranted in the statement "that the universal
struggle for existence, having succeeded in bringing forth
that consummate product of creative energy, the Human Soul,
has done its work and will presently cease.   In the lower
regions of organic life it must go on, but as a determining
factor in the highest work of evolution it will disappear."+
And Professor Huxley, we believe, correctly summarizes the relation of the human struggle for existence to the survival of
the truly fittest in the propositions that the ethical man
"devotes his best energies to the object of setting limits to
the struggle", that "the history of civilization * * * is the
record of the attempts which the human race has made to es-

* Same reference as the last.
+ The Destiny of Man, pp. 96-97.

cape" from the struggle, and that the most perfect society is
the one in which the struggle is most strictly limited.*

(3) Considered as a test of mere physical fitness,
"natural selection" unaided by intelligent intervention is
painful, wasteful and slow.

It does not secure the survival of all the (physical-
ly) fit, but of only a small part of them.   Even "cold-blood-
ed scientists" plead guilty to a shudder as they regard the
inconceivable waste and agony that must have marked the age-
long track of advancing evolution.   The wastefulness of the
process has been largely due to the following causes.

(a) Destruction of the immature superior by the mature
inferior.

(b) Destruction of a small number of superiors by a
larger number of inferiors.

(c) Destruction of a more highly organized species by
a tougher species.

(d) Destruction of the fittest of any species by the
fortuities of nature (flood, famine, lightning, cold, etc).
Without intelligent intervention an analagous waste, propor-
tionally painful and extensive will be produced by analagous
causes.   "When we come to human beings in society, the State
is the chief instrument by which waste is to be prevented.

* Article—"The Struggle for Existence",Nineteenth Century,
  February, 1888, pp. 165-166.

53

The mere struggle for existence between individuals means
waste unchecked. The State by its action can in many cases
consciously and deliberately diminish this fearfuly loss; in
many cases by freeing the individual from the necessity of a
perpetual struggle for the mere conditions of life, it can
set free individuality and so make culture possible.   An i-
deal State would be one in which there was no waste at all of
the lives, and intellects, and souls of individual men and
women."*

From these facts we believe the conclusion to be an
easy one that "the teaching of evolutionary science, rightly
understood, gives us no excuse for putting aside all schemes
of social reorganization as mere foolish and dreamy idealism."+

We believe that the following propositions against
the theory of laissez-faire have been sustained.

1.   As a theory of liberty it is self-contradictory
in practice.

2.   The inequalities of opportunity that are most per-
sistent are unalterably established before the individual powers upon which laissez-faire stakes the issue are maturely developed.

3.   It over looks the quasi-public character of some

* D.G.Ritchie- Principles of State Interference,p. 50.
+ D.G.Ritchie,-Darwinism and Politics,-p.26.

of the most oppressive restraints upon industry.

4.   It ignores the fortuitous inequalities of supply
and demand.

5.   It is vitally dependent upon a number of false
assumptions.

Therefore it is not the principle upon which society
must organize in order to secure the best industrial liberty.

3rd.   State-Action.

This theory admits of brief statement.   It holds that
the State should intervene in industrial affairs whenever
and to whatever extent such intervention will promote the
general welfare of society, the propriety of every such act
being judged by the probable consequences of the intervention.

We will consider,

1.   The argument in favor of this theory.

2.   The argument against it.

1.   The theory may be maintained as follows:

a.   The general welfare of society, while in dispute
as a matter of ethical theory, is not particularly in dispute
as a matter of practical good.   As to how the summum bonum
shall be defined, philosophers differ;   but no sane man denies
that economic comfort, intelligence, health, friendship, mor-
ality, etc., are good for every human being.   Equality of op-

portunity, as an industrial ideal is to be the particular
test of social welfare applicable here.

b. It is possible for legislatures, after due study
and discussion, to determine in most cases whether or not
any given measure will promote the general welfare (including
industrial liberty). This proposition requires the proof of
two subordinate propositions.

(a) The subjects of legislation to be dealt with are
subjects within the range of human knowledge. Social phenomena have not been studied as thoroughly as they ought to be
and will be, but it will hardly be contended by anyone that
the subject itself is outside the range of human investiga-
tion, or that the results of State-intervention are such as
can never by any available degree of prudence be foreseen.

(b) The men who legislate upon these subjects are men
who are able in most cases to reach correct conclusions. at
any rate, they are as competent to determine to act as to determine not to act. Mr. Spencer thinks otherwise,*but his
arguments amount substantially to saying that because legislators have in the past most frequently made mistakes, they
are bound to continue to do so. This argument will be presently criticised. Let it be said here that State-action in
approximate democracies like our own, is based on the almost
* See "The Sins of Legislators" in The Man vs. the State.

56.

56.

axiomatic proposition that the majority of men in the majority
of cases are more likely to act wisely than unwisely. Otherwise, human intelligence would be only a mockery and the is-
sues of life as well decided by a toss of the dice as by the
deliberations of the reason.

2.   Several arguments urged against this principle
will now be considered in detail.

a.   It is argued that expediency is an indeterminate
standard- that it amounts to saying that what is good is good.*

This argument is open to the general criticism that it
ignores the distinction between the theoretical summum bonum
and the practical categories of desirable things, the former
being indeterminate but the latter not. Many may differ, for
instance, as to why happiness is good, but they do not dispute that it is good.

Mr. Spencer however gives two reasons definite and
plausible at least, for regarding expediency as an indefinite
test.

(1)   He urges first, the fact that different individuals have different standards.+   To this it may be replied
that the general welfare is not to be promoted by enabling
each individual to attain his own standard of well-being, but

* See H. Spencer,-Social Statics, pp. 11-28, and Chap. XXII,
  section 5 (Appleton's Edition.)
+ Social Statics- Introduction- Section 2.

rather in so influencing his character as to elevate his standard of welfare.   But how are we to know that one conception
of welfare is more "elevated than another?   Simply by the fact
that the more intelligent men become, the more do they value
of certain things (as, for instance, benevolence), and the
less other things (as gratification of the appetites).

(2) Mr. Spencer urges the further fact that the same
individual at different periods of his life will adopt different ideals of welfare.*   True; but the riper judgment of
maturity would rarely hesitate to declare which of the two
was the true ideal.

Mr. Spencer would have us adopt as the criterion of
legislation, instead of an empirical utilitarianism his own
evolutional utilitarianism,- that is, to legislate, not with
regard to particular supposed consequences, but with regard
to fundamental generalizations derived from all human experience.+   On the contrary, we believe these "generalizations"
to be more indefinite than expediency.   Every generalization
includes an almost infinite possibility of less general generalizations. Are we to follow only the most general principles conceivable?   If so, how general must our formulae be
made in order that they cannot be made more so?   Or shall we
take account both of the widest and all less wide generaliza-

* Same reference as the last.
+ The Great Political Superstition, in The Man vs. the State.

tions? If so, we must approach indefinitely near to individual cases, which would be practically the empirical standard
of utility.

b.   For statement and criticism of another objection
I can do no better than quote the words of one often quoted
before in this discussion.

"In the essay on' The Sins of Legislators', Mr. Spencer
appears to maintain that, because governments in the past
have made great errors, therefore they can never be trusted
to do well; because sumptuary laws were mistaken, sanitary
legislation is mischievous.   Is there not such a thing as
learning by blunders in individual life?   And may not a nation learn in the same way?   Because we have been unsuccess-
ful hitherto in one direction, are we to give up every attempt
in other directions?   'To behave well, do nothing at all',
thought Hans, the awkward youth in the German story; and Mr.
Spencer appears to think with him.   I might as well argue
that because (in Mr. Spencer's opinion) all philosophers in
the past have been mistaken, therefore Mr. Spencer must be
mistaken also. On the other hand, he argues that, since inventions have been made and trade has grown and languages have
been developed without the State doing anything, government
action should not be much esteemed.   I might perhaps similar-

ly argue that, because all these good things have come about
without the aid of Mr. Spencer's philosophy, therefore Mr.
Spencer's philosphy is of little worth; but I am aware that
such a mode of argument is fallacious, and think it more important to raise the question, whether all these good things
have happened without the help of the State?   Mr. Spencer's
inductions, derived presumably from tables of descriptive sociology, remind one of the story(referred to by Bacon) about
the votive offerings hung up by those who had escaped ship-
wreck, nothing being said about those who had been drowned.
Mr. Spencer's historical scraps are like those votive offerings.   The ill successes of English sanitary legislation are
recounted, but nothing is said about those countries which
have no sanitary legislation at all.   It is true, that where
there are no drains at all, there can be no typhiod fever produced by bad drains;   in the good old days before sanitary
legislation they had the plague instead.   'Uninstructed legislators', we are told, 'have continually increased human suffering in their attempts to mitigate it.'   Of course we do
not know what blessed results might follow from legislators
brought up on Mr. Spencer's writings, or perhaps from hereditary legislators in whom the whole system of synthetic philosophy had by descent acquired the character of relatively a
priori truth.   We can only compare countries that we actual-

ly know about; and though doubtless our uninstructed legislators have blundered frightfully, yet, we think, on the whole,
we are not so badly off as some people who have never had Par-
liaments to blunder at all.   Let us improve our legislature,
educate our legislators, codify our laws, by all means; but
it is childish to argue that, because three thousand Acts of
Parliament have been repealed, it is a mistake to pass any.
If your clothes do not fit you, that is no reason for going
naked.   If the State had done nothing in the past, we should
be infinitely worse off, and we should not know so well the
evils we have to remedy. It is nonsense to speak as if legislation in the past had been one continued failure.   Many
of these Acts of Parliament have been repealed, not because
they are useless or mischievous, but because they have proved
so useful that new Acts have been passed extending their principles and applications or consolidating previous legislation
on the subject.   In any case, Mr. Spencer surely cannot deny
the advantages States have conferred on trade by coining money, opening up roads, making harbors, providing lighthouses,
etc. If he questions this, let him only consider the conditions of trade in places where the State, being in a rudimen-
tary stage, has done nothing of the sort.   Of course, some
people might argue that men were better off without trades,

but I do not think Mr. Spencer would take that line."*

In this connection note a striking inconsistency of
Mr. Spencer- He sees a certain providence, not to be rashly
meddled with, in the failures of experiments made by individuals.+ He holds that they result in the elimination of the
incapables, the accumulation of instructive experience, warn-
ing to society, stimulus to caution, etc., and so are to be
reckoned among the good things of evolution. But of the
failures of collective action he assumes that they will have
contrary results. Would it not be more consistent with the
evolution theory to regard these legislative failures simply
as the unhappy but instructive variations in the process of
political selection?

But where shall a line be drawn- how shall we determine when we have had enough laws?   Simply as we determine
when we have had enough dinner,- as Professor Huxley suggests§
by the symtoms.

c.   It is argued that the interference of majorities
is just as tyrannical as the interference of monarchs, since
the oppression depends, not on who interferes, but on the
mere fact of the interference.#

─────────────────────────────────
* D.G.Ritchie, Principles of State Interference, pp. 53-57.
+ See Social Statics, p. 413 ,(Appleton's Edition.)
§ Administrative Nihilism (Humboldt Edition) p. 42.
# H. Spencer- "The Great Political Superstition" in The Man
  vs. the State.

62

We answer, - the oppression lies rather in the character and aim of the interference. If it seeks, as is too apt to be the case with a monarch, simply the gratification of governing individuals at the expense of the public, it is tyranny. But if it seeks the welfare of the public at the public expense, it is no tyranny even though some of the public object. Of course it is possible that a selfish majority may seek their own gratification rather than the common good, and do so at the minority's expense rather than the common expense. What security then have we against such "tyranny of majorities?" None that is absolute, two that are practical. (1) The rule of majorities comes the nearest possible to identifying the interests of the governed with the interests of the governing power. (2) It is safer to trust the rights of the individual to the average conscience of a majority than to the single conscience of a monarch. One man is more likely to do wrong than a majority of men are to conspire together to do so.

Certainly there is no taint of "divine right" in this doctrine, nor is there even rhetorical license for calling these tangible and obvious propositions, "the great political superstition."*

Mr. Spencer tries to set an inflexible limit to the authority of majorities. He argues that the majority has the

* See last chapter of The Man vs. the State.

right to control the minority only in those matters in which
all have agreed to be controlled.   These matters are such
interests as concern all in common, and grow out of the very
laws of life.   (1) In order to procure means of subsistence
man must have freedom to move about within the limits set by
the equal freedom of others. (2) When division of labor obtains, he must have freedom of exchange and contract, together with protection against fraud or breach of contract.   In
these respects it is assumed that men have agreed to submit
to government and in no others.*

Here is a tissue of assumption and conjecture. It is
certain that government did not come into being as the result of any such compact or any compact at all, but simply as
an extension of the patria potestas.+   And never has, and
never can or could, any such conpact be made.   Until the day
when laws are no more needed, there will be found an irrecon-
cilable minority who refuse to submit to such laws as they
choose.   Surely Mr. Spencer has given us nothing but a (somewhat) revised edition of Rousseau's "Contract Social" and
here at last "the great political superstition" is found.

Mr. Spencer himself admits that this agreement as to
undisputed functions of the State is only a "practical unanim-

---

* See "The Great Political Superstition" in The Man vs. the
  State, Also Social Statics, Chapter XVIII.
+ See W. Bagehot—Physics and Politics, Chapter I, Section II.

ity." * That is to say, criminals, Quakers, etc., are to
be left out of the practical account in declaring the agreement unanimous and practical unanimity is to consist of disre-
garding small minorities. But exactly how small must they be
in order to be left out of account? Oh, very small!

A further security against the tyranny of majorities
and particularly of their legislative and executive represent-
atives is to be had in some such constitutional device as
the admirable system of "checks and balances illustrated in
the government of the United States,+ together with a minute
division of functions and decentralization of power.§ Indeed
there can be but one principle upon which even a "practical
unanimity" can be reached,— the principle that the common weal
shall be sought in every way which an actual majority shall
deem advisable.

d. Mr. Spencer tells us further that "All socialism
is slavery". (In "Socialism" he here includes all State-intervention.) He defines slavery as "involuntary labor for
another" and socialism as involuntary labor for the State."#

Slavery is indeed involuntary labor for another, but
the definition includes much that is not slavery. Most of

* The Man vs. The State, p. 85
, See L. M. Cooley,—Checks and Balances in Government.
§ See D.G.Ritchie-Principles of State Interference,p. 10, and
  Sir F. Pollock- History of the Science of Politics, p. 123.
"The Coming Slavery" in The Man vs. The State.

every man's labor in involuntary because if he will not work,
he shall not eat, and often such involuntary labor is for a-
nother, as when a man's works support his own family. A
rather more accurate definition would be: slavery is the absence of exforceable rights to the product of one's labor or
its equivalent utility.   And just such slavery is possible
when the wages- contract is made between two unequal "industrial units".   It is such slavery as this that laissez-faire
ignores and State- Action seeks to abolish as far as possible.

E. The State has been defined as "men voluntary asso-
sociated for mutual protection "and it is argued that to as-
sign it other functions violates the principle of division of
labor, thus impairing its efficiency in the discharge of its
primary functions.*

To this objection we reply:

(1) Government is either a solely protective agency
or it is not. (a) If it is, it has still two imperative du-
ties.   First, to protect its subjects- Second, to protect
itself in order to protect its subjects.   This second duty
warrants not only the war-function, but many such "interferences", as public education,+ State-boards of arbitration,etc.
(b) But government is promotive as well as protective. Negative functions may have been the earliest that were exercised

* H. Spencer-Social Statics,p.303 (Appleton's Edition.)
  Cf.J.S.Mill-Principles of Political Economy,Book V,Ch.XI,§4.
+ See H.Spencer-Social Statics,pp.304-305(Appleton's Edition.

by the State, but equally critical necessities must soon have
called forth other activities which were just as natural feat-
ures of social evolution as the perhaps earlier ones; as, for
instance,- co-operation in hunting expedition, or today in
postal service.

     f.   It is objected to State-Interference that society
is an organism and that to tamper with its natural growth will
only cause malformations.

     This objection is based on the arbitrary distinction
already discussed (see infra,p. 71-73) between "natural" and
"artificial" influences.   It is indeed true that "Constitutions are not made but grow."   But how do they grow?   By
variation and selection.   Must these variations and selections
occur unconsciously and spontaneously, according to the strict
biological analogy, as Mr. Spencer assumes,* or consciously,
according to intelligent purposes and by means of wise legislation?

     Indeed if social laws are fixed as biological laws there
can be no fear or possibility of their violation, and as we
have further seen, there can be no "artificial" phenomena in
a law-ruled universe.

     g.   Against State-action it is argued that "the man
who is in every point fitted to his circumstances * * * cannot

---

* Social Statics, Chapter XXII, section 3.

be helped. To do anything for him by some artificial agency
is to supersede certain of his own powers."*

Can the perfect man be helped?   Suppose he desires to
send a letter to a distant friend. He must employ some one
to carry it for him; why should not the government be employed?   In any case some one must help him.

And what of such children as may be said to be per-
fectible, but whose parents fail to give them due care?   Is
it only with the mature that society is concerned?

Nor has "the man perfectly fitted to his circumstances"
yet appeared.   Very well, Mr. Spencer would say, he will come
the sooner by leaving imperfect men to struggle with their
environments until the friction shall wear them into harmony.
But why must the man yield to the environment rather than the
environment to the man.   Perfection is something more than
adaptation to environment, else we must call the gorilla a
more perfect being that Socrates;   perfection is rather adaptation to a good environment,-thatis, an environment which
affords incitement and assistance to the attainment of the
highest mental and moral ideals.   Meanwhile, the imperfect
man can be helped by giving him, as nearly as possible, an
environment to which it will be perfectly desirable to have
him perfectly conformed.

* H. Spencer- Social Statics (Appleton's Edition) pp. 308-309.

h.   It is said that State-action would be subversive of individuality.*

"It may very well be doubted whether absence of control would necessarily produce individuality, at least such individuality as constitutes ' an element of well-being.'   As a matter of history, do we find that the growth of a settled State system and the elaboration of laws are adverse to the existence of individuality? A tribe of savages or barbarians are all very much more like one another than a similar number of civilized men of the same country.   Among civilized men there is a much greater variety of facial expression than among those at a lower stage.   What certainly is true is, that in earlier times, when locomotion was more difficult in the world at large, or in any given country, there was a more picturesque diversity.   The inhabitants of one province or town differed more from that (sic) of another; but within each of these smaller areas it may be very much questioned whether there was as much scope for individuality as there is now.   The man who differed from his neighbors too much ran a greater chance of exile or death than in times when the areas over which the same law prevails are larger.+

1.   It is said that State-interference is usually resorted to as an opiate, to relieve pain, unmindful of the fact

* J.S.Mill- Liberty- Chapter III.
+ D.G.Ritchie- Principles of State Interference, pp. 88-89.

that most suffering is remedial.

Granted that suffering is a good social remedy, legislation may still have the character of a prophylactic rather than an opiate.   And is it not true that even when remedying past evils, pain often sows the seed of future ones?

It is also said that suffering is often deserved by
and so diciplinary to the sufferer.   But would it not be better if we could so alter a man's circumstances as to make him
feel less incitement to violate the laws of nature and thus
require this painful dicipline.

Our practical conclusion concerning State-action is
that the State should intervene in industrial affairs whenever
the results of such particular intervention seem to promise
greater equality of opportunity to the members of society.

4th.   Socialism.

Socialism may be defined as State-owner-ship of the
means of production, State-control of the processes of production, and State- distribution of the products of production.

An elaborate discussion of this important theme is not
to be attempted here.

Socialism in the strict sense differs from State-action
in that the former holds that intervention is desirable in e-

very industrial process, while the latter holds that better
results may often, and perhaps most often be obtained at present by non-intervention. Against socialism as an immediate
policy, State-action clearly holds the field, since it is
generally admitted even by Socialists, that the only way of
putting their theory into actual realization is to bring the
phenomena of industry one by one into the gra-dually widening
sphere of State-action.

VI. Specific Measures as Related to
Industrial Liberty.

Sixth question: How shall the principle of State-action be applied to specific purposes?

The following tests of each proposed action seem sufficient to determine its expediency.*

First: Will the end desired contribute to equality
of opportunity?

Second: Will the means proposed secure the object
desired?

Third: Can the object be attained without greater
cost than its worth?

We have already discussed by way of illustration several proposed measures of "interference". Such further discussion of these as we now undertake will likewise be illus-
* D.G.Ritchie-Principles of State Interference,pp.108-109;
  Also Sir J.F.Stevens, Liberty, Equality and Fraternity,p.54,
  (2nd Edition.)

trative rather than exhaustive.

1st. Public Education.

We will consider first the public school system, as-
suming this system to be what is understood by the words"free"
and "compulsory". Let these tests be applied.

1. Does popular intelligence promote the best industrial liberty? An affirmative answer is supported by two
considerations.

a. It promotes the liberty of the one who receives
the education by affording opportunity for the development
of his powers as nearly equal as possible to the opportunity
afforded to others. Mr. Spencer would deny this. "Omitting
instruction", he writes, "in no way takes from a child's freedom to do whatever it will in the best way it can; and this
freedom is all that equity demands."* This proposition lends
itself to a reductio ad absurdum. For instance, tying a man's
hands in no way takes from a man "freedom to do whatever he
will in the best way he can"- with his hands tied. To circumscribe his intellectual faculties limits his freedom just
as truly as to circumscribe his sphere of locomotion. Again
Mr. Spencer asks: "If there should be an act of parliament
for the development of their minds, why should there not be
an act of parliament for the development of their bodies?"+

* Social Statics- Chapter XXVI, section 1.
+ Social Statics, Chapter XXVI, section 2(Appleton's Edition)

72

Indeed there is such an act; children whose bodily needs are
not provided for by their parents, like those whose parents
fail to educate them, are cared for by the state.

   b.   Not only is the intelligent man himself freer than
the unintelligent, but his intelligence contributes to the
freedom of the community in that he is less likely through
pverty, crime, or otherwise, to become an occasion of public
expense.*

   So far as the prevention of vice is concerned, Mr.
Spencer has flatly denied any efficacy to education.+ However, he hardly seems to have convinced anybody and has con-
ceded that if education could be efficiently applied to the
emotional nature, it would then easily serve to promote moral-
ity.§   Modern educational systems certainly seem disposed
to give due attention to the emotional natures of children,
and so far as successful herein, take all the force out of
Mr. Spencers objections.

   2.   Are the means employed (free and compulsory education) adequate to secure the end desired (popular intelligence)?

   It has been said that State -education is an artificial
effort to unify those faculties which nature has made diverse.#

* T.H.Huxley- Administrative Nohilism,p. 39(Humboldt Edition).
+ Social Statics, Chapter XXVI, Section 9(Appleton's Edition.)
§ Social Statics, Chapter XXVI, Section 9(Appleton's Edition).
# J.M.Bonham, Industrial Liberty, p. 291.

73

'But in bringing up children in State schools, are you not moulding their opinions in a particular groove, and is not that interfering with freedom of opinion?' If the State were minutely to direct and control the education of the universities, or even of the secondary schools, there might be some reason for asking this question. But is Mr. Spencer really afraid of a theological bias being imparted by means of the multiplication table,- of a metaphysical system being introduced into the A, B, C, and of a Tory twist in the formation of pot-hooks? The freedom of opinion of those who cannot read and write, and will not let their children learn, does not seem to be a very precious thing."

3. Finally we ask, Does the end obtained by the public school system involve greater sacrifice than it is worth?

An affirmative answer has been given on two grounds,viz:

a. "First, that it is inconsistent with the principles of a free government to enforce a policy which begins with an unequal exaction from the citizens— a policy which declares that A shall be responsible for the schooling of B's offspring, and that part of A's industry shall be exacted from him for this purpose."+

---

* R.G.Ritchie- Principles of State-Interference, p.117.
+ J.M.Bonham, Industrial Liberty, p. 291.

74

This objection is just as applicable to the protection of individuals from violence.   A, who has no children, is taxed for school purposes ten times as much as B who has ten children.   Likewise A, who never invokes the remedies of the law, is taxed ten times as much as B, who frequently does. It may be said that both A and B alike share the state of good order secured by the existence of government.   But the same is true of the similar benefits of popular intelligence.

b.   "Second, that it is likewise inconsistent for the government by arbitrary interference to assume the father's duty."*

And why should not the State "assume the father's duty" if the father abdicates his duty or is unable to perform it?   For the sake of both, society ought to protect itself and the child from the consequences of the father's ignorance, superstition, selfishness, or incapacity.

2nd.   Sanitary Supervision.

Boards of Health, quarantine measures, drainage and sewage systems, compulsory vaccination, etc., have been challenged as infringements of liberty.

1.   Does good health contribute to equality of opportunity?

* J.M.Bonham, Industrial Liberty, p. 291.
+ H. Spencer, Social Statics, Chapter XXVIII.

75

We can see no distinction relevant to our subject between protecting a man from mayhem and protecting him from
contagious disease.   Or why protect property and not health.
Property gives its possessor opportunity to secure his industrial interests;   likewise does good health.   But to
protect his health is said to interfere with "the process
of adaptation",* while to protect his property is said to
promote it.+

    2.   Are the measures in question suited to promote
the desired end- the protection of public health?

    Mr. Spencer devotes five of the most interesting pages
of his Social Statics to recounting the eggregious failures
that have accompanied the attempts of the State at sanitary
supervision.§   And after he has said his worst, one is bound
to reflect that the very intelligence with which Mr. Spencer
discusses the theme is proof positive, not that these bad results are necessary consequences of sanitary supervision,
but that Mr. Spencer has so clearly set forth the particular
errors to be avoided, that sanitary supervision can at last
proceed securely toward its ends.   The discussion on pp.
26, 27, 30 (infra) is pertinent at this point.

* H. Spencer Social Statics, p. 431.
+ H. Spencer, Social Statics, Chapter X.
§ Social Statics, Chapter XXVIII, Section 6.

76

Mr. Spencer further objects to the means employed, on the ground that no definite scope can define their operation,- that they logically warrant legislation regarding the minutest hygienic details of personal habit which would require an army of executive officers to enforce to any apparent degree.*

To this it may be answered that two practical limits are possible.   a.   The sanitary supervision of the State must not be carried so far as to withdraw needed energies from other and equally important functions.   b. It must not extend so far in protecting the individual's health as to correspondingly impair his other interests, as privacy, economy, etc.

3.   Is the end desired obtainable by the means proposed without too great a cost?

Mr. Spencer promptly replies: "Inconvenience, suffering, and death are the penalties attached by nature to ignorance, as well as to incompetence—are also the means of remedying these.   * * * But to guard ignorant men against the evils of their ignorance— to divorce a cause and consequence which God has joined together— to render needless the intellect put into us for our guidance— to unhinge what is,

* Social Statics- Chapter XXVIII, Section 2.

in fact, the very mechanism of existence- must necessarily
entail nothing but disasters."*

The fact is here ignored that if we "divorce a cause
and consequence" we necessarily do so by means of another
cause of equally divine origin.   Certainly an intelligent
purpose intelligently pursued is as divine and natural a cause
as an unconscious fortuity.   And it is, further, not merely
a question of protecting an ignorant man from the consequences
of his own ignorance, but of protecting whole communities
from plagues which show no more respect to the persons of the
intelligent and good, than to the brutish and evil.   No, this
imagined interference with divine law is not too great a price
to pay for the object desired.   The laws of hygiene like the
law of economics "are statements of tendencies expressed in
the indicative mood, and not ethical precepts in the imperative."+

3rd. Prohibition of the Liquor-Traffic.

1.   The abolition of the use of alcoholic liquors (as
a beverage) would contribute to the best industrial liberty
of several classes of people. a.   Those who drink; by economy of faculties and wealth, thus giving them greater industrial opportunities. b.   The families of those who drink;

---

* Social Statics, pp. 412 and 413 (Appleton's Edition.)
+ Marshall, Principles of Economics, Preface, p. VI.

by economy of their means of subsistence. c. Society at
large; by diversion of material resources from destructive
to reproductive consumption.✱

   2.   Is the means suited to the end?   This is a
mooted question.   Suffice it to say here that if the liquor
traffic is ever entirely abolished it must be some other policy than licenses or regulations which in themselves pre-sup-
pose its continued existence.

   3.   Will it require too great a cost?   Not if one-
tenth of the crime, disease, poverty and waste attributed to
this industry are justly chargeable thereto.

   4th.   "Protective" Tariffs.

   1.   The aim of these measures is to afford profit to
industries which would be unprofitable if not so aided by the
State.   This hardly seems consistent with industrial liberty.
It is manifest that whatever amount of wealth the State be-
stows upon such industries must have first abstracted by the
State from other industries.   Therefore it takes from one
what he has earned in order to give another what he has not
earned and what it is not necessary to the former's welfare
that the latter should have (as in the case of school taxes),
and is an explicit contradiction of equalized opportunities.

_____

✱ See F.A.Walker- Political Economy, Section 347.

79

The commonest apology for this practice is that it enables
the "protected"industry to offer employment to labor, and so
maintains a high rate of wages.

2.   We therefore inquire, Is this result actually secured by the system?   It is obvious that the ability of
"protected" industries to employ labor is increased only to
the extent of the funds thus bestowed upon it and it is e-
qually obvious that the ability to employ labor of the industries from which these funds are abstracted must be decreased
to an exactly equal extent.   Therefore, the system stands
condemned by the second as by the first test.

5th.   <u>Policy toward Corporate Monopolies.</u>

Concerning all corporate monopolies involving "trust"
relations, the valuable proposition has been made that there
should be legal recognition and enforcement of a double trust
relation, treating not only the shareholders, but the com-
monwealth as well as cestuis que trustent.*

This suggestion rigidly and universally applied would
alone amount to almost another industrial revolution.   The
two-fold oppressions, both of employes and consumers would
be almost abolished if not entirely.

---

* See J.M.Bonham- Industrial Liberty, pp. 150-158.

80

Summary.

The present perior of history is distinctively an industrial period and consequently efforts for human liberty
are now directed to the attainment of industrial rather than
political or religious liberty(infra, pp. 1-4).

Liberty, considered negatively, is immunity from absolute co-ercion and from hindrances and influences unfavorable to desirable choices; considered positively, it is the
enlargement of personal opportunities and powers. (infra pp.
5-15)   The problem of industrial liberty is concerned with
all those social phenomena which condition human freedom in or
through the economic relations of men(infra pp. 15-16).

Absolute liberty is impossible to finite beings, Whatever liberty there is must be in the realm of volitional
freedom; beyond that necessity is the exceptionless rule
(at least so far as anything less than Divine Power is concerned).   Discussion of our present subject is meaningless
on the hypothesis of determination. Therefore moral freedom
is assumed. (infra pp. 16-19.)

The largest industrial liberty would not be afforded
by anarchy, which is the negation of liberty, nor by laissez-
faire which is only anarchy minus unrestricted violence and

treachery, nor by independence, which is contrary to man's
social nature, but in equal interdependence among "industrial
unites". (Infra pp. 20-37.)

Such an absolute equal interdependence would remove
the necessary stimulus of individual development and therefore
though it is the largest, is not the best industrial liberty.
Equality of opportunity is the ideal.   (Infra pp. 37-47.)

Equality of opportunity will not be most perfectly
secured by Anarchy, laissez-faire, or entire and immediate
socialism, but by intelligent State-action seeking specific
and desirable ends (together with the influence of individual
altruism.   (Infra pp. 47-106.)

The relation of equality of opportunity to specific
measures of State-activity is illustrated by public policy,
actual or proposed, concerning education, sanitary supervision, the liquor traffic, the "protection" of domestic industries, and corporate monopolies. (Infra pp. 107-120.)

Appendix.

Bibliography.

Banks, L.A.--White Slaves.

Bonham, J.M.-- Industrial Liberty.

Ely, R.T.-- Outlines of Political Economy.

Ely, R.T.-- Socialism and Social Reform.

Graham, W.-- Socialism: New and Old.

Gunton, G.- - Principles of Social Economics, Part IV.

Huxley, T.H.- - Administrative Nihilism.

Jevons, W.S.- - The State in Relation to Labor.

Mill, J.S.- -Liberty.

Mill, J.S.- - Principles of Political Economy, Book V, Chap-
                  ters I and XI.
Montague- -The Limits of Individual Liberty.

Owen, W.C.- - The Economics of Herbert Spencer.

Pembroke- - Liberty and Socialism.

Ritchie, D. G.- Darwinism and Politics.

Ritchie, D.G.- Principles of State Interference.

Salter, W.M.- Anarchy or Government.

Spencer, H.- The Man versus the State.

Spencer, H.- Principles of Sociology.

Spencer H.- Social Statics.

Stephen, Sir J.F.- Liberty, Equality, Fraternity.

Toynbee, A.- Ricards and the Old Political Economy.

Wagner, A.- Grundlegung der Politischen Ockonomie.